CHRISTO AND JEANNE-CLAUDE

THROUGH THE GATES AND BEYOND

JAN GREENBERG AND SANDRA JORDAN

A NEAL PORTER BOOK

ROARING BROOK PRESS

NEW YORK

To my three Graces
Lilly, Coco, and Clara
— *JG*
To my friend and mentor
Ann K. Beneduce. The Best!
— *SJ*

CHRISTO: *Wrapped Roses, 1967-92*

Copyright © 2008 by Jan Greenberg and Sandra Jordan

A Neal Porter Book
Published by Flashpoint, an imprint of Roaring Brook Press
Roaring Brook Press is a division of Holtzbrinck Publishing Holdings Limited Partnership
175 Fifth Avenue, New York, NY 10010

Designed by Pam Glaven
Impress, Inc., Northampton, MA

Distributed in Canada by H. B. Fenn and Company, Ltd.

Library of Congress Cataloging-in-Publication Data

Greenberg, Jan.
Christo and Jeanne-Claude : Through the Gates and Beyond / Jan Greenberg and Sandra Jordan.
p. cm.
"A Neal Porter book"
Includes bibliographical references.
ISBN-13: 978-1-59643-071-6
ISBN-10: 1-59643-071-0
1. Christo, 1935 – 2. Jeanne-Claude, 1935 – I. Christo, 1935 – II. Jeanne-Claude, 1935 – III. Jordan, Sandra. IV. Title. V. Title: Christo and Jeanne-Claude.
N7193.C5G74 2008
709.2'2--dc22
2007019951

10 9 8 7 6 5 4 3 2 1

Roaring Brook Press books are available for special promotions and premiums.
For details, contact: Director of Special Markets, Holtzbrinck Publishers.

Printed in China
First edition October 2008

Christo and Jeanne-Claude, Japan, 1988

1
THE GATES
CENTRAL PARK, NEW YORK CITY
1979–2005

"We have never done a sad work."
Christo

"Most human beings are afraid of what is new.
It is our work to convince them that they will
enjoy it, and even if they don't, to allow us just
for sixteen days to create a work of art."
Jeanne-Claude

In the winter of 2005, Christo and Jeanne-Claude
became two of the most visible artists in the world,
gracing the covers of magazines from New York
to Japan. What had riveted the world's attention?
The Gates, Central Park, New York City, 1979 – 2005,
the largest work of art ever created for the largest
of all American cities, was about to be completed
with great fanfare. Seventy-five hundred and three
shimmering saffron panels would be unfurled in
New York's Central Park. Would *The Gates* cause
celebration or controversy?

BACK IN 1979 what were the chances of Christo and Jeanne-Claude constructing a giant artwork stretching 23 miles through Central Park? After all, Central Park is New Yorkers' big backyard, the place where they run, bike, walk dogs, play ball, skate, and even take rides in horse-drawn carriages. It has acres of green grass. Thousands of stately trees. Long curving paths, a lake, ponds, fountains, a castle, a zoo, sculptures, and a merry-go-round. The mayor was skeptical of the artists' proposal. Some environmentalists worried about it damaging the park's trees, plants, and wildlife. In 1981, the Parks Commissioner published a 185-page book saying "no."

But Christo and Jeanne-Claude never give up easily. All of their grand-scale outdoor works of art are the result of countless meetings with countless people over long periods of time. Talking to the public about their concerns is part of the artistic process, and issues —

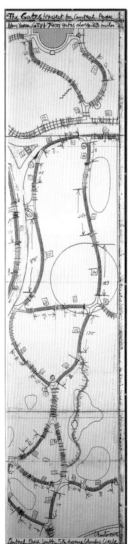

CHRISTO: *The Gates,*
Project for Central Park,
New York City.
Drawing 2002 in two parts

from the environment to safety and the use of the site —
are incorporated into the work. Getting a yes took energy,
persistence, and 26 years. Finally, in 2003, the artists signed
a 43-page contract with the city allowing *The Gates* to go
forward. The long wait was over. On February 12, 2005,
Christo and Jeanne-Claude would transform Central Park
into one huge work of art.

Who would pay for such an ambitious undertaking?
The artists accept neither sponsors nor public money.
All outdoor projects are financed by the sale of Christo's
"indoor" artworks — including collages, drawings, scale
models, and some early works.

For months Christo holed up in his studio, often spending
15 hours a day making preparatory drawings. Downstairs,
Jeanne-Claude fielded telephone calls and organized
thousands of details. As creative partners, the artists
worked together in a whirlwind of activity.

Steel for the bases was manufactured at ISG
steel mill in Pennsylvania. *(left)*
Special saffron nylon fabric was woven at the
Schilgen plant in Germany *(center)*, then sewn
and cut into panels. *(right)*

15,006 steel bases are put into place at previously
determined locations. *(top)*
Aluminum corner sleeves are inserted into the tops
of the vertical poles and bolted in place. *(center)*
The gates are assembled. *(bottom left)*
The bases are leveled. *(bottom right)*
The gates are elevated
and bolted onto the
bases. *(far right)*

Usually an artist labors in the studio and exhibits a finished artwork in a museum or gallery. But *The Gates* would be erected in Central Park while the whole world watched.

In January of 2005, 15,006 mysterious looking black steel boxes were spaced roughly every 12 feet along the miles of paths in the park. These boxes were actually solid bases, an ingenious solution to the problem of supporting the posts without digging holes in the grass or walkways.

On February 6, six days before *The Gates* was scheduled to open, 600 workers, paid by Christo and Jeanne-Claude, fanned out across the park in teams of eight. They confirmed that the black boxes were level. On the bases they put up tall, saffron-colored poles made in a factory for that project. Tightly wrapped banners extended across the tops, ready to be unfurled.

The public became more and more curious.

Television and newspaper commentators argued back and forth. It seemed as if everyone had an opinion. Why would these two artists spend millions of dollars to create a gigantic artwork that would remain for only two weeks?

Was it art?
What did it mean?
Why did they do it?

When questioned, the artists always insist that they make their art to please themselves. Jeanne-Claude says, "Artists paint apples because they have the urge to paint apples. And if people like the art, that's a bonus."

Now *The Gates* would snake through Central Park, offering a fiery burst of color on a bleak winter landscape. It was Christo and Jeanne-Claude's 21-million-dollar gift to their adopted city.

You had to be there to see it.
You couldn't wait.
Because in 16 days it would all disappear.
The stage was set for opening day.

2

CHRISTO AND JEANNE-CLAUDE
SERENDIPITY

"The art world jokes about us,
Christo is so nice and gentle,
and he always says yes to everybody.
Then he sends me to say no."
Jeanne-Claude

MAYBE IT WAS MERE COINCIDENCE, but people
who know Christo and Jeanne-Claude prefer to call it
fate. Born thousands of miles apart on the same day, in
the same year, June 13, 1935, they were destined to
meet, marry, and together change the way the world
thinks about art. Their childhoods were very different,
his in Bulgaria and hers in Morocco, France, and
Switzerland. But after 1939, both were affected by the
calamity of the Second World War.

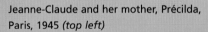

Jeanne-Claude and her mother, Précilda, Paris, 1945 *(top left)*

Christo (in hat) and his older brother, Anani, in the garden, Gabrovo, Bulgaria, 1945 *(top right)*

Christo, his older brother, and mother, Tzveta, Gabrovo, 1939 *(center left)*

Drawing lesson, Christo at far right, Art Academy in Sofia, 1949 *(center right)*

Jeanne-Claude holding her son, Cyril, born May, 1960 *(bottom left)*

Jeanne-Claude and Christo in his studio, Manhattan, 1970 *(bottom right)*

CHRISTO JAVACHEFF WATCHED his mother burning the family's treasured modern art books, frightened that the military authorities in Bulgaria would consider them cause for arrest. Meanwhile, Jeanne-Claude's mother, Précilda, was eager to join French patriots fighting against the Germans. Although her parents had separated before she was born, six-year-old Jeanne-Claude was left in Morocco with her father's family. After the war, Précilda reclaimed her daughter and moved to Paris. There the glamorous Précilda married a French officer and brought up her daughter in a life Jeanne-Claude says was filled with "parties, pretty clothes, and tennis."

After Germany lost the war, Christo attended schools run by the country's new Communist government. Art students found themselves assigned to make propaganda materials — posters glorifying the revolution or portraits of political

CHRISTO: *Wrapped Cans and a Bottle, 1958–59 (left)*
CHRISTO: *Wrapped Road Sign, 1963 (right)*

leaders. Only the Communist Party doctrine was tolerated. If Christo took anything from the lessons of these school days it was the concept of community spirit, with artists playing an active role in bringing people together.

What the young artist didn't want was the State looking over his shoulder, telling him what he could or could not create. He yearned for freedom, enough to risk his life for it. When he was only 21, while visiting Prague, the capital city of Communist-dominated Czechoslovakia, he crept on board a freight train and huddled for hours in a freezing boxcar to escape across the heavily guarded border into Austria. There he would be able to make art his own way. Later his artwork with Jeanne-Claude became, in their words, "a scream for freedom."

But even a free man has to eat. Christo painted portraits to support himself, signing them with his family name, Javacheff. His real art, the art that mattered to him, he signed with his first name — Christo. At that time his work consisted of crumpled envelopes he encrusted with layers of resin and glue. The wrinkled and layered effect would lead to his first wrapped objects, or "packages." These mysterious objects (often bottles or cans), covered in a canvas soaked with resin (a liquid that dries hard and clear) and elaborately tied with twine, were a breakthrough for Christo. With their deliberately concealed contents, the small parcels speak of secrets, a hidden life. They have a humble quality both in material and appearance.

Eventually, in 1958, Christo found his way to Paris. There he met Jeanne-Claude's mother, Précilda, who hired him to paint portraits of herself and her family. She didn't count on her strong-willed, vivacious daughter falling in love with the impoverished artist. After Christo and Jeanne-Claude's son Cyril was born, the small family's finances were strained to the limit, but Jeanne-Claude says, "We were never poor, we were just temporarily without money." They existed on soup made from bones and bruised vegetables purchased cheaply from the market. Art became their shared passion.

When he was promised a solo exhibition in Germany, Christo began to wrap feverishly. Oil barrels and wooden crates, yes, but also a chair, their bedside table, Jeanne-Claude's dress, her favorite shoes, and Cyril's toy horse.

By then Christo and Jeanne-Claude were working as partners — collaborating — on the grand-scale outdoor artworks. *Wall of Oil Barrels, Rue Visconti, Paris, 1961 – 62* was a large piece they created together, though at the time it was credited to Christo. Jeanne-Claude says there were enough problems persuading the public to accept their new ideas without confusing them with the equally new idea of two artists' signatures.

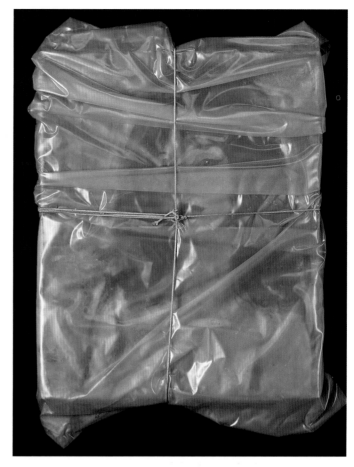

CHRISTO: *Wrapped Portrait of Jeanne-Claude, 1963*
(top right)
CHRISTO: *Package on a Wheelbarrow, 1963*
(below left)
CHRISTO: *Wrapped Toy Horse, 1963*
(far left)

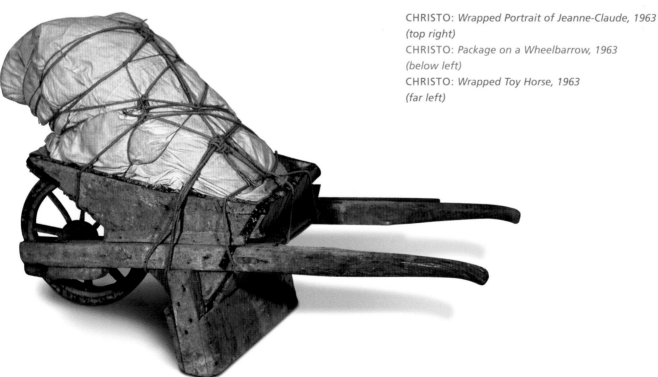

The plan was to build a temporary wall of barrels across a narrow Parisian street on the Left Bank, a district supportive of artists. Traffic would be stopped for hours, so the artists needed a government permit. Barrels were assembled, trucks hired, invitations to art-world figures mailed, but no permit arrived. Christo and Jeanne-Claude decided not to let that stop them.

At 6:30 PM on June 28, 1961, Christo began unloading the barrels while Jeanne-Claude managed the crowd. To construct the wall according to their careful plan took only 30 minutes, but the first policeman arrived before it was finished.

"It's a work of art," Jeanne-Claude explained to the unconvinced gendarme. Darkness fell. The cheerful crowds and flashing lights from cameras gave the scene a festive atmosphere. At midnight, Christo and the trucker began to take the barrels down. By one in the morning, the wall had vanished as if it had never existed. Yet the success of *Wall of Oil Barrels* deepened Christo and Jeanne-Claude's belief in the idea that artworks can be temporary and not made to last forever.

Drawn by the innovative art scene, in 1964 the artists moved to New York City, where they dreamed of wrapping skyscrapers and museums. Their works became larger and larger, including the Store Fronts, sculptures that could take up almost the whole floor space of a gallery. They planned projects from Australia to France. But wherever the artists went, they fiercely guarded their independence.

Christo and Jeanne-Claude during the installation of *Running Fence,*
Sonoma and Marin Counties, California, 1972–76

3

EVERY PROJECT
TELLS A STORY

"All of our projects have this fragile quality. They will be gone tomorrow.
They have total freedom. That is why they cannot stay.
Because freedom is the enemy of possession and possession is equal to permanence.
We have to have freedom with no strings attached."
Christo and Jeanne-Claude

WHETHER THE PROJECT involves a fence crossing ranches full of curious cattle or wrapping the most historic bridge in Paris in fabric and rope — a rural or an urban site — what Christo and Jeanne-Claude's projects have in common is that, like a rainbow or a beautiful sunset, they are short-lived. When the artists are asked why they put so many years and so much money into something with a planned life span of about two weeks, they reply that for the last 5,000 years artists have used many materials and qualities in every imaginable way, "but there is one quality they have never used, and that is the quality of love and tenderness that we, human beings, have for what does not last."

The artists plan for years. They hold public meetings. They commission environmental and engineering reports. Safety tests are performed. All the parts and pieces are manufactured to their exacting design. Then, usually for no more than two weeks, throngs of people flock to see these large-scale works of art. Afterward, the art is removed and the materials recycled. Reactions of viewers vary from delight to disbelief. But the projects never fail to surprise, each one different, with its own shape, size, geography, time span, and materials. And each one tells its own story.

VALLEY CURTAIN, 1970–1972

A curtain made of orange woven nylon fabric, suspended on four steel cables about 1,500 feet long, anchored to the mountaintops on foundations

Christo and Jeanne-Claude chose Rifle Gap, a cleft in the mountain outside a small mining town in Colorado, for the site of *Valley Curtain*. The list of technical problems to overcome was challenging. Nothing like *Valley Curtain* had ever been attempted, so there were no models to follow. In October 1971, after months of delays, the curtain was set to go up. But just as the crew raised the orange curtain two-thirds of the way, the contractor called a halt to work for the day, concerned that approaching darkness threatened the crew's safety. By dinnertime part of the bright orange fabric began unraveling from a slight breeze. By daylight the next morning it hung shredded and still, a total loss. At the press conference the

"Pull!" yelled Christo.

following day, the citizens of Rifle gave Christo and Jeanne-Claude a standing ovation. The artists promised the town they would be back. Less than a year later, on August 10, 1972, Christo and Jeanne-Claude stood ready to unfurl the new curtain. "Pull!" yelled Christo. "Pull, pull, pull, pull!" The vast cloth billowed open. Like a giant butterfly, it fluttered and spread its orange wings. Christo beamed. "Beautiful!" 28 hours later, a high wind clocked at more than 60 miles an hour swept down and reclaimed the valley. The curtain was destroyed. Despite the *Valley Curtain*'s brief life span, Christo and Jeanne-Claude were satisfied. They had realized their dream.

"Pull, pull, pull!"

RUNNING FENCE, 1972–1976

An 18-foot-high, 24.5-mile-long fabric fence passing through 59 ranches in Sonoma and Marin Counties, California

After *Valley Curtain*, Christo and Jeanne-Claude set out to complete another ambitious project — a glowing white-fabric fence that would cross two counties in Northern California. It was so difficult to get the necessary permissions from government agencies and environmental groups that *Running Fence* seemed impossible. But the artists have an uncanny knack for drawing people into the process.

There were 18 public hearings in 1974 – 1975, and the opposition to the artists was organized and vocal. Far from being discouraged, Christo and Jeanne-Claude stood up during the heated public debate and told the crowd that the whole process, including the enemies, the supporters, the hearings, the studies, and the petitions — and not just the fence they hoped to build — were all a part of the art.

One by one, the obstacles were overcome. The ranchers became the artists' enthusiastic supporters. The final installation took crews four days to complete. It would remain for two weeks. Christo, watching the *Running Fence* swelling in the ocean breeze, said it "gives shape to the wind."

24

SURROUNDED ISLANDS, 1980–1983

Eleven islands in Biscayne Bay, Florida surrounded with 6.5 million square feet of pink woven polypropylene floating fabric

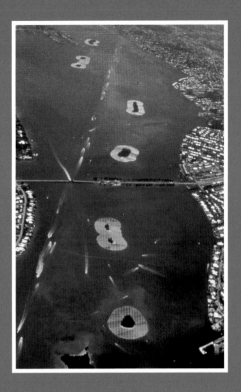

In 1980 the artists traveled to Miami, Florida looking for a possible site for a project. Nothing inspired them until they stood on a bridge looking at the small manmade islands that dot Biscayne Bay. It was Jeanne-Claude who suggested surrounding them with pink fabric that would float on the water. They chose 11 islands, and the artists began the time-consuming and difficult process of getting approval from the many city and government agencies involved. Environmentalists worried about birds that nested on the islands and endangered manatees that lived in the warm, shallow waters. Eventually, approval was granted. Usually the artists return a site to its original condition, but this time they improved it by removing 40 tons of garbage.

For two weeks in May 1983, the specially woven flamingo-pink fabric floated and extended out from each island. Light, land, and water blended in a harmonious whole.

WRAPPED REICHSTAG, 1971–1995

1.076 million square feet of woven polypropylene fabric with an aluminum surface and ten miles of bright blue polypropylene rope wrapped around the Reichstag in Berlin, Germany

It took 24 years to get permission to wrap the Reichstag, the once and future seat of parliamentary government in Germany, built in 1894 and almost destroyed in 1945. The artists went to Germany more than 50 times to meet with six successive presidents of the German Parliament.

More than five million people experienced the *Wrapped Reichstag*, the building shrouded in a silvery woven polypropylene fabric and ten miles of rope. The building, transformed for two weeks by the artists, became a symbol of democracy in a reunited Germany.

"When Christo's hair turned gray and mine turned red, we

Carrying out such monumental works requires dedication, patience, and the organizational skills of a general. Since the beginning of their collaboration, Christo and Jeanne-Claude had been, as one friend observed, "an eagle with two heads." In 1994 they finally announced that they were making official what anyone who knew them already realized. The outdoor projects created since 1961 would be officially credited to them as joint artists.

decided we were mature enough to tell the truth," says Jeanne-Claude.

4
EVERY DRAWING
HAS A HISTORY

"I've drawn all my life, since I was a little boy of six.
I love to draw and make collages…but the beauty,
the force, the energy of these works come from…
the particular moment in which I drew them."
Christo

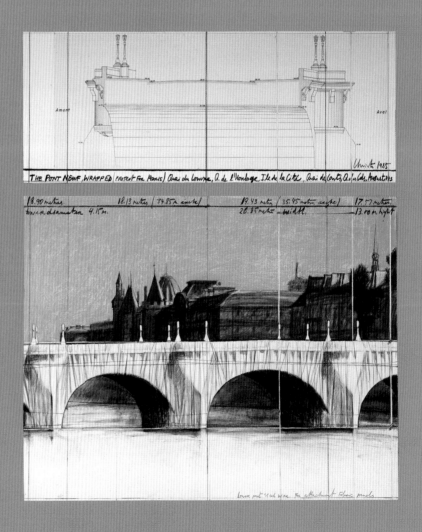

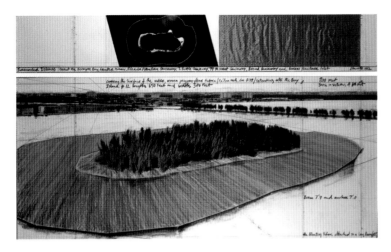

CHRISTO: *The Pont Neuf Wrapped, Project for Paris.*
Collage 1985 in two parts (far left)
CHRISTO: *Surrounded Islands, Project for Biscayne Bay,*
Greater Miami, Florida. Drawing 1982 in two parts (left)
CHRISTO: *The Gates, Project for Central Park,*
New York City. Collage 2004 in two parts (right)

UP A STEEP STAIRWAY inside the no frills brick warehouse where the artists have lived and worked for over 45 years waits Jeanne-Claude, smiling, her face haloed by her trademark mane of red hair. Christo, slim, gray-haired with a wry, elfin look, stands at the door. On the walls of a spare white room are Christo's large preparatory drawings for *The Gates*. In a soft French accent, punctuated by an easy laugh, Jeanne-Claude explains that Christo does all the drawings, "because I can't draw." Christo makes his drawings, without the help of even one assistant, and signs them Christo. (Outdoor works of art are credited "Christo and Jeanne-Claude.") His studio hasn't been painted since 1964. He says he is too busy to bother. There is a table to make collages and a wall for large drawings. Although the artist usually stands, sometimes he puts on kneepads and works on the floor. Because it takes time for the glue to dry, he often works on several collages at a time. When a piece is completed, Christo sprays it with fixative and puts it in a Plexiglas frame.

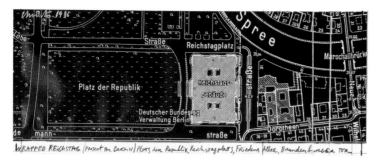

Jeanne-Claude says, "Drawings are very important to us because they tell the story of every project." The first drawings for *The Gates* in New York City were made in 1979. They are records of the way a project changes and grows. Even though Christo has piles of unfinished drawings, he never destroys any of them. However, Jeanne-Claude points out that once a project is completed, "Christo does not create any more drawings."

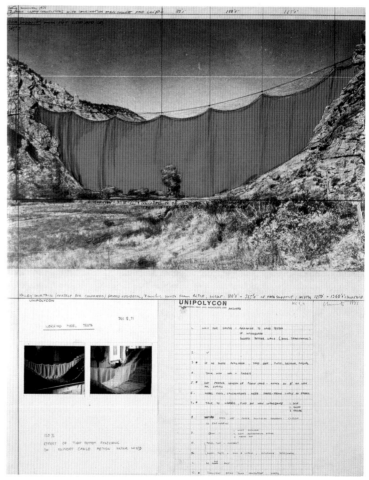

CHRISTO: *Valley Curtain, Project for Colorado. Collage,* 1971 *(right)*
CHRISTO: *Wrapped Reichstag, Project for Berlin. Collage 1986 in two parts (top left)*
CHRISTO: *The Umbrellas, Joint Project for Japan and U.S.A. Drawing 1991 in two parts (bottom left)*
Every day, Christo walks up five flights of stairs to work in his studio. New York City, 1991 *(far right)*

5
ENTER THE GATES

"Nobody can buy these projects.
Nobody can own these projects.
Nobody can charge tickets for these projects.
Even we do not own these projects."
Christo and Jeanne-Claude

Aerial view of part of *The Gates (left)*
CHRISTO: *The Gates, Project for Central Park,
New York City. Drawing 2004 in two parts
(right)*

FIVE, FOUR, THREE, TWO, ONE! As crews unfurl each saffron fabric panel into the freezing February morning, the crowd cheers. Thousands of people are gathered to watch teams of workers, dressed in gray uniforms with "The Gates" emblazoned in bright orange, spread out across Central Park and set the panels free. Surrounded by Mayor Bloomberg, officials of New York, and other well-wishers, Christo and Jeanne-Claude laugh with joy. Like fluted columns, the nylon fabric panels seem to stand in silence for a moment…then, with a gust of wind, they float back and forth in swaying rhythms.

"Look at the colors, the light," says Christo. "It's like a painting." A painting with nature as its canvas!

The Gates follows the 23 miles of walkways, from 59th Street across from the fabled Plaza Hotel up to 110th Street in Harlem. It spreads in ripples of brilliant saffron, weaving, circling through the footpaths of the great park…in and out…up and down, crisscrossing and rising. Old linden, oak, and maple trees hover, their bare branches forming skeletal patterns against the blue sky. The New York City skyline rises beyond the park. From grand brick and limestone buildings and hotels on Central Park South, spectators can get a bird's-eye view of the saffron canopies. The artists say, "They [are] like a golden river appearing and disappearing through the bare branches."

New York City mayor Michael R. Bloomberg opens one of the first gates with Christo and Jeanne-Claude beside him. *(left)*
Enter *The Gates*. *(right)*

"People enter Central Park in a ceremonial way. It is surrounded by a stone wall," says Christo. "There are many entrances, each called a gate by the landscape architects, Frederick Law Olmsted and Calvert Vaux, who designed the park. *The Gates* is a very ceremonial project, a festive project." Once the gates are completely unfurled, a parade of people march through them from one end of the park to the other.

"The fabric has a dynamic quality," says Christo. "All our projects are like living objects. They are in continuous motion all the time, moving with the wind."

The weather affects the way we experience *The Gates*. On some days the sky is flat and gray and the fabric panels hang solidly against the dark sky. On other days the sky is blue and the wind is blowing — the panels flap and wave, and seem

to glitter in the bright light. Rain, snow, sunshine, each change in the weather gives us a new view of the work.

People fly in from all over the globe. Hotels in Manhattan are filled, the restaurants booked. For 16 days, it seems as if everyone in New York is trying to find the words to describe what they saw and felt. But young or old, rich or poor, New Yorker or tourist, art lover or skeptic, they all have something to say about the artwork in the park!

"It touches people. And it makes people happy."
"The Gates reminds me of Samurai warriors, their orange banners raised, marching through the park."
"I come every day. My favorite was the day it snowed. My dog liked it, too."

"**THE GREATEST SURPRISE** of a project," says Jeanne-Claude, "is that when it is completed it is a million times more beautiful than our wildest dreams." Those who use the park all the time and take it for granted find themselves noticing the details with a fresh eye — the stone arched bridge, the copper beech trees, the reflection of the gates in a half-frozen pond, the birds, gray rock formations.

Jeanne-Claude asserts again and again, "It has no purpose. It is not a symbol. It is not a message." During their many trips to the park, when fans surround the artists, asking them to pose for photographs, Jeanne-Claude in her direct way instructs them to look at *The Gates,* not at her and Christo.

Then suddenly it's over. After 16 stunning days, workers begin to remove the artwork. By the middle of March, as promised by the artists, the materials are hauled away, the steel bases melted down to be recycled, the aluminum used for cans of soda, the fabric shredded and made into carpet padding. The vinyl poles are also recycled. The artists do not sell any part of *The Gates* to private collectors or museums. When spring arrives a few weeks later, and flowering trees blossom in the park, no trace of *The Gates* remains, except in our memories, the photographs, books, a film, and countless articles.

Christo likes the expression "once upon a time." He has said, "Once upon a time, *The Gates* were in Central Park." Jeanne-Claude has something else on her mind: "As soon as *The Gates* come down, we will continue working on our next project."

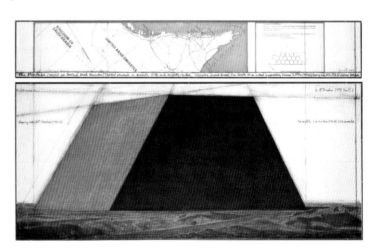

CHRISTO: *The Mastaba, Project for the United Arab Emirates. Drawing 2007 in two parts*

In the United States, since 1992, the artists have proposed suspending 5.9 miles of silvery fabric panels horizontally above 40 miles of the Arkansas River in Colorado. For two weeks in July and August of 2012, it will be possible to view *Over the River* from the highways and to experience it by raft and kayak. Imagine the adventure of gliding down the river under a shimmering roof, as if on a journey to a mythic place.

Meanwhile, on the other side of the world, the artists continue to develop a challenging plan for an artwork. *The Mastaba of Abu Dhabi, Project for the United Arab Emirates*, will be made of 410,000 oil barrels. The brightly colored oil barrels, objects used by the artists in some of their earliest work, refer to the source of the country's wealth. It will stand both wider and taller than the largest pyramid in Giza, Egypt. Final permits have yet to be granted, but given the success of *The Gates* and Christo and Jeanne-Claude's passion and perseverance, it seems likely that another dazzling transformation will unfold to amaze us.

We'd love to be there.
Wouldn't you?

CHRISTO: *Over the River, Project for Arkansas River, State of Colorado. Drawing 2006 in two parts*

THE GATES
SOME STATISTICS

CHRISTO AND JEANNE-CLAUDE became familiar with every inch of the 23 miles of paths their gates traversed. Most of the gates were sited and then spaced 12 feet apart, but sometimes an overhanging branch or low-growing tree made an adjustment necessary. Not even one branch was trimmed, tree roots were avoided, and rock formations were respected. All proceeds from the sale of posters, mugs, T-shirts, sweatshirts, and other memorabilia went to support nature protection foundations.

CHIEF ENGINEER AND DIRECTOR OF CONSTRUCTION: Vince Davenport
PROJECT DIRECTOR: Jonita Davenport

To put up 7,503 gates took the following materials, which were manufactured to Christo and Jeanne-Claude's exacting specifications: 7,503 gates, 16 feet high. The width varies from 5'6" to 18 feet, depending on the width of the path.

- 315,491 LINEAR FEET of recyclable saffron-colored vinyl tubing, to make the five-inch square vertical and horizontal poles

- 5,290 TONS of steel to make 15,006 steel bases that weigh 600 to 800 pounds each, to make certain that each gate was stable

- 15,006 cast-aluminum corner reinforcements

- 165,000 bolts and self-locking nuts

- 116,389 MILES of saffron nylon thread to make 46 miles of hems

- 7,503 panels made of woven nylon, a highly reflective synthetic fabric

ISG steel mill in Pennsylvania.

SELECTED PROJECTS

For a complete list see the website: http://www.christojeanneclaude.net

1961

■ *Dockside Packages, Cologne, Germany*
Christo and Jeanne-Claude's first collaboration.

1962

■ *Wall of Oil Barrels, Iron Curtain, Rue Visconti, Paris*

1968

■ *Wrapped Fountain and Wrapped Medieval Tower, Spoleto, Italy, 1961–68*
■ *Wrapped Kunsthalle, Berne, Switzerland, 1967–68*
■ *5600 Cubicmeter Package, Documenta IV, Kassel, Germany*

1969

■ *Wrapped Museum of Contemporary Art, Chicago, Illinois*
■ *Wrapped Floor and Stairway, Museum of Contemporary Art, Chicago, Illinois*
■ *Wrapped Coast, Little Bay, One Million Square Feet, Sydney, Australia*
One-and-a-half miles of seacoast, wrapped with one million square feet of Erosion Control Mesh (synthetic fabric), and 35 miles of polypropylene rope. The coast took four weeks to install and remained wrapped for ten weeks before being restored to its original condition.

1970

■ *Wrapped Monuments, Milan, Italy*

1972

■ *Valley Curtain, Grand Hogback, Rifle, Colorado, 1970–72*

1974

■ *The Wall, Wrapped Roman Wall, Rome, Italy*
■ *Ocean Front, Newport, Rhode Island*

1976

■ *Running Fence, Sonoma and Marin Counties, California, 1972–76*

Wrapped Coast   Wrapped Walk Ways

1978

- *Wrapped Walk Ways, Loose Park, Kansas City, Missouri, 1977–78*
  This installation of apricot-colored nylon fabric covered 2.8 miles of walkways and jogging paths for two weeks.

1983

- *Surrounded Islands, Biscayne Bay, Greater Miami, Florida, 1980–83*

1985

- *The Pont Neuf Wrapped, Paris, France, 1975–85*
  This temporary (14 days) work of art of woven polyamide fabric, silky in appearance and sandstone in color, covered the sides, vaults, and parapets (down to the ground) of this 17th-century bridge over the river Seine in Paris, France. Also covered were the sidewalks and curbs, the street lamps on both sides of the bridge, the esplanade of the Vert-Galant, and the vertical tip of the Île de la Cité, an island in the middle of the Seine.

1991

- *The Umbrellas, Japan and USA, 1984–91*
  3,100 umbrellas, each 19 feet, 8 inches high and 28 feet in diameter, opened the same day in two inland valleys an ocean apart — 1,340 blue ones in a 12-mile-long valley in Ibaraki, Japan, and 1,760 yellow ones in an 18-mile-long valley in Tejon Pass, California.

1995

- *Wrapped Reichstag, Berlin, Germany, 1971–95*

1998

- *Wrapped Trees, Foundation Beyeler. Berower Park, Riehen, Switzerland, 1997–98*
  178 trees located in the park and in the adjacent meadow were wrapped with 592,034 square feet of woven polyester fabric (used in Japan to protect trees from frost and heavy snow) and 14.35 miles of rope. The park dates back to the year 1551.

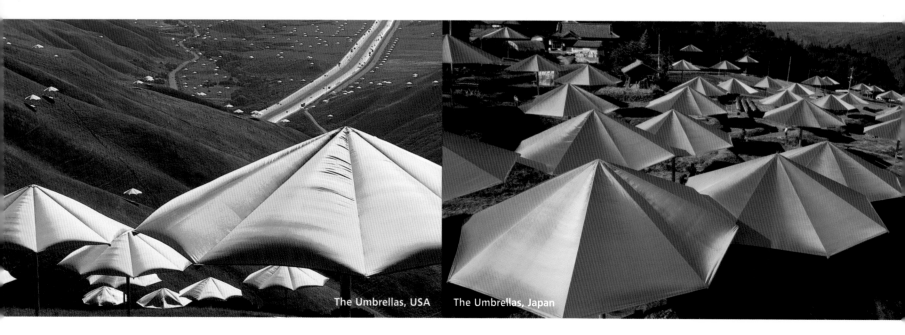

The Umbrellas, USA   The Umbrellas, Japan

AUTHORS' BIBLIOGRAPHY

WEBSITE: Christo and Jeanne Claude: http://www.christojeanneclaude.net

BOOKS

Bourdon, David, and Alexander Tolnay. *Christo and Jeanne-Claude: Early Works 1958-1969*. New York: Taschen, 2001.

Chernow, Burt. *Christo and Jeanne-Claude: A Biography*. New York: St. Martin's Press, 2002.

Christo, and Jeanne-Claude. *The Gates: Project for Central Park, New York City*. Westport, CT: Hugh Lauter Levin Associates, Inc., 2003.

Donovan, Molly. *Christo and Jeanne-Claude in the Vogel Collection*. National Gallery of Art, Washington, D.C. New York: Harry N. Abrams, 2002.

Fineberg, Jonathan. *Christo and Jeanne-Claude: On the Way to The Gates, Central Park, New York City*. The Metropolitan Museum of Art, New York. New Haven: Yale University Press, 2004.

Vaizey, Marina. *Christo*. New York: Rizzoli, 1990.

ARTICLES

Barron, James. "Dressing the Park in Orange and Pleats." *New York Times*, February 13, 2003.

Confessore, Nicholas. "Some Sadder Than Others as First 'Gates' Start Falling." *New York Times*, March 1, 2005.

Kimmelman, Michael. "In a Saffron Ribbon, a Billowy Gift to the City." *New York Times*, February 13, 2003.

Kinetz, Erika. "It Isn't Public Until They Say It Is." *New York Times*, February 16, 2003.

Plett, Nicole. "Christo & Jeanne-Claude: Unwrapped." *U.S. 1 Newspaper*, February 19, 1997. Also available at http://www.princetoninfo.com/christo.html.

Sternbergh, Adam. "The Passion of the Christos." *New York Magazine*, January 24-31, 2005.

Tansini, Laura. "Inside the Gates." *Art on Paper*, April 2003.

Vogel, Carol. Inside Art. *New York Times*, June 6, 2003.

Weisman, Steven R. "Christo's International Umbrella Project." *New York Times*, November 13, 1990.

FILMS

Christo and Jeanne-Claude: The Gates. Antonio Ferrera, Albert and David Maysles, Matt Prinzing, 2008.

Christo and Jeanne-Claude: Dem Deutschen Volk (Wrapped Reichstag). Wolfram and Jorg Daniel Hissen, EstWest, 1996.

Christo and Jeanne-Claude: Wrapped Trees. Wolfram and Jorg Daniel Hissen, EstWest, 1998.

Christo in Paris. Albert and David Maysles, 1990.

Christo's Valley Curtain. Albert and David Maysles/Ellen Giffard, 1972.

Islands. Albert and David Maysles, 1985.

On the Way to Over the River. Wolfram and Jorg Daniel Hissen, EstWest, 2006.

Running Fence. Albert and David Maysles/Charlotte Zwerin, 1977.

Umbrellas. Albert Maysles, Henry Corra, and Graham Weinbren, 1996.

Wrapped Coast. Blackwood Productions, 1969.

Wrapped Walk Ways. Blackwood Productions, 1978.

NOTES

Quotes from the authors' interviews except for the following:

PAGE 5   "We have never done...." (artists' website)

PAGE 5   "Most human beings are afraid...." (artists' website)

PAGE 15   "We were never poor...." (Chernow p. 95-96)

PAGE 18   "It's a work of art...." (Chernow p. 109)

PAGE 21   "All of our projects...." (Chernow p. 272)

PAGE 23   "'Pull!' yelled Christo...." (*Valley Curtain* film)

PAGE 24   "Gives shape to the wind...." (*Running Fence* film)

PAGE 30   "I've drawn all my life...." (Laura Tansini, "Inside the Gates," *Art on Paper*, April 2003, p. 45)

PAGE 32   "Drawings are very important...." (Tansini p. 45)

PAGE 39   "Look at the colors...." (*New York Times*, "Central Park Dresses Up as Orange Pleats Unfurl," February 13, 2005)

PAGE 39   "They [are] like a golden river...." (artists' website)

PAGE 40   "People enter Central Park in a ceremonial way...." (http://www.princetoninfo.com/christo.html)

PAGE 41   "It touches people...." (*New York Times*, "Central Park Dresses Up as Orange Pleats Unfurl," February 13, 2005)

PAGE 42   "Once upon a time, *The Gates* were in Central Park...." (*New York Times*, "Central Park Dresses Up as Orange Pleats Unfurl," February 13, 2005)

PHOTO CREDITS

All photographs © Christo and Jeanne-Claude
All photo permissions courtesy of Christo and Jeanne-Claude
Jacket Wolfgang Volz
Pages 1, 4, 6, 8, 9, 10, 15, 17, 18, 24-25, 26, 27, 28-29, 30, 31, 32 *left, top* and *bottom*, 33, 34, 36, 38, 39, 40-41, 42, 43, 47, 47, 49 Wolfgang Volz
Page 2 Andre Grossmann
Page 13 *top left* Jacques de Guillibon; *top right, center left* Vladimir Yavachev; *bottom left* Wjera Fechheimer; *bottom right* Harry Shunk
Pages 14, 17 Eeva-Inkeri
Page 16 Dirk Bakker
Page 19 Jean-Dominique Lajoux
Page 20 Gianfranco Gorgoni
Pages 22-23, 32 *right*, 42 *left*, 46 *left* Harry Shunk

ACKNOWLEDGMENTS

There are many people to thank for their help in making this book possible. First of all, heartfelt appreciation to the artists Christo and Jeanne-Claude, not only for their amazing artwork, but also for their time, generosity, and patience with the book process; to Wolfgang Volz for his handsome photographs; to Richard Edwards and the late Harley Baldwin for their introduction to Christo and Jeanne-Claude; and to Jonathan Henery and Vladimir Yavachev of Christo and Jeanne-Claude's studio for their help in practical matters. We are also grateful to the many people young and not-as-young who walked *The Gates* with us from one end of Central Park to the other and shared their thoughts and impressions — the Avram and Rohatyn families, Nancie Jordan, Katie Weisberg, the Finn-Foleys, Ronnie Greenberg, Jackie Greenberg, Samantha Verrone, Sofie and Aaron Somarov, Gay Elwell, Ralph Elia, and Kristin and Chris Vila. Turning a manuscript into a book takes many hands, and gratitude goes to the erudite George Nicholson, the ineffable Neal Porter, the multi-talented Simon Boughton, inventive designers Pam Glaven and Hans Teensma at Impress, Inc., ever vigilant Laaren Brown, Jennifer Van Dalsen, blessedly efficient Kat Kopit, and last but never least, the resourceful Lauren Wohl.

LIST OF ARTWORKS